THE RED BALLOON

'*This adaptation, derived from both the film and slim tie-in book, captures the spirit, look and feel of the original and movingly expresses them in stage terms*' **Guardian**

'*If there is a more charming and magical children's musical I haven't seen it...Clark's clever and sensitive adaptation is backed by a haunting and tuneful score by Mark Vibrans that ranges from taxing choral pieces to touching solos.*' **Manchester Evening News**

'*Messing with masterpieces is a risky business...Yet for all the turkeys there are a handful of triumphs.* My Fair Lady *is one;* The Red Balloon *another. Whether it's the embodiment of an imaginary friend, a symbol of innocence, experience or even death, the balloon's significance is never explained which is the reason for its overwhelming resonance.*' **The Financial Times**

Mark Vibrans' score, with echoes of Satie, introduces strong themes which then return to cumulative effect, and provides at least a couple of tunes which you can remember well enough to whistle days afterwards...My general rule with kids' shows is to watch the audience to see how rapt the tinies are being kept. This time I forgot, too intent on the stage myself. Kids' theatre too often looks as though it's constructed from a theatre's leftover budget, actors and ideas; this one has clearly been put together with dedication and effort. The best show I've seen anywhere in the past six months.' **City Life**

'*The way that children torment each other and parents harangue their offspring is acutely observed in this memorable and beautiful adaptation...Nothing about this falls short of excellence.*' **Time Out**

The Red Balloon at the Royal National Theatre, 1996

Anthony Clark

THE RED BALLOON

adapted for the stage from a film by
Albert Lamorisse

Book and lyrics: Anthony Clark
Music: Mark Vibrans

OBERON BOOKS
LONDON

First published in 1999 by Oberon Books Ltd
(incorporating Absolute Classics)
521 Caledonian Road, London N7 9RH
Tel: 020 7607 3637 / Fax: 020 7607 3629
e-mail: oberon.books@btinternet.com

From a film by Albert Lamorisse 1956
Stage adaptation and lyrics by Anthony Clark
Music by Mark Vibrans, available upon request from Oberon
Books Ltd

A catalogue record for this book is available from the British
Library.

ISBN 1 84002 079 2

Author photograph copyright © Bill Cooper

Cover illustration: Danusia Schejbal

Frontispiece copyright © Gautier Deblonde

Series design: Richard Doust

Printed in Great Britain by MPG Ltd, Bodmin

Contents

For Anna, Gabriel, Eleanor and Crispin

INTRODUCTION

Anthony Clark

In 1953, Albert Emanuel Lamorisse, director, scenarist, cinematographer and producer began work on his fourth short film *Le Ballon Rouge*. A perfectionist, it is reported that he wrote forty-two versions of the script before he was satisfied with it. The film tells the story of Pascal, a lonely child who is bored at home, and ignored by his classmates, until he makes friends with a large red balloon. The film has no words, and stars Albert's five-year-old son. The film was shot in Eastman colour, but printed on Technicolor stock, which gives it its Utrillo-like ethereal aura. It was released in 1956, and was an immediate success with audiences and critics. Jean Cocteau called it, 'a fairy tale without fairies', and a British reviewer wrote that 'it lends stature to the cinema as a whole.' It won many prizes including *Medaille d'Or du Grand Prix du Cinema Français*, and the *Palme d'Or* at the Cannes Film Festival. It has become a classic.

In 1957 Albert Lamorisse published the story in written form accompanied by stills from the film.

In 1989 I adapted the story from book and film for the stage, with a brief to stick closely to the spirit of the original. I chose a musical form because the story is simple and resonant, emotionally. Mark Vibrans, with whom I have collaborated on numerous occasions, wrote the score. The text and score have been developed over four productions: first at Contact Theatre (1989), then at the Bristol Old Vic (1990), Birmingham Repertory Theatre (1995) and finally at the Royal National Theatre (1996). I would like to thank the casts, the designers Kendra Ullyart and Ruari Murchison, and the three choreographers, Lorelei Lynne, David Massingham and Malcolm Shields, for their contribution to this adaptation.

The Balloon: I don't know how they did the balloon in the film, and there may be more ingenious ways of realising it than mine. This is how I did it: I got a large, strong, red, round, helium-filled balloon; attached a lightweight stiff cord (dressing-gown cord) to its nozzle, sellotaped one end of a couple of metres (the armspan of the operator/puppeteer) of invisible thread (fishing line) 20cm from the nozzle, passed the other end of the line through a hole at the end of a thin, strong wooden rod, just under a metre in length, and tied it to the end of another rod of similar length. The operator/puppeteer held the rods in his/her hands. By placing the rod with the hole wherever the operator/puppeteer wanted the balloon to go, and pulling or releasing the tension on the line with the other rod, it was possible to control the balloon's movements and give the illusion of independent flight.

At one point in the text the balloon is required to write on a blackboard. This was done by attaching a small piece of chalk to the rod with the hole at the end. This rod was placed right under the nozzle of the balloon by pulling the line away with the other rod. Thus it was possible to mask the chalk. At the end of the story the balloon should 'die' very slowly. After losing lots of balloons, we discovered the best way to do this: after the 'pack of children' had all fired their catapults at the balloon, they would rush Pascal who was holding the balloon, triumphantly, and mask him while he cut a very small hole near the nozzle of the balloon with a pair of nail scissors. They then broke away from Pascal as he released the balloon, and watched it deflate. The effect is moving, and capable of creating an extraordinarily tangible silence in the theatre.

The Revolt of the Balloons, in the closing minutes of the musical, was done equally simply. Fishing lines were attached to various points on the set and stretched to hidden points in the auditorium. Balloons with weighted strings (large curtain rings did the trick) were then sent down the lines and collected by the cast. The strings were pulled through the curtain rings by the cast and handed to Pascal. Where flying was available flying wires were attached to Pascal while he was surrounded by hundreds of floating balloons and he then took off, to spontaneous applause.

The Company: This musical can be performed by as few as eleven actor-singers or as many as you like. I saw it produced in Holland in 1998 with fifty children and two adults, to great effect.

Anthony Clark, 1999

THE RED BALLOON

Characters

RED BALLOON

PASCAL

LAMPLIGHTER

TRAMP

MAMAN

PAPA

ALBERT
a caretaker

MLLE ELAINE
a teacher

HEADMASTER

GIRL
in the white dress

BUS CONDUCTOR

PICTURE SELLER

CYCLE SELLER

PHOTOGRAPHER

BLUE BALLOON

SCHOOL CHILDREN AND PEOPLE OF PARIS

A version of this script of *The Red Balloon* was first performed at the Contact Theatre, Manchester, in December 1989, with the following cast:

Louise Yates, Amelia Bulmore, Jane Cox, Philip Rham, Claude Close, Kieran Cunningham, Andy Crooks, Rachel Spry, Chris Garner, Jane Lancaster and Philip Aldridge.

The Royal National Theatre cast included: Nicky Adams, Malcolm Shields, Jane Howie, David Rubin, Rashan Stone, Lucy Dixon, Nigel Betts, Naomi Radcliffe, Daniel Crowder, Joanna John, Natasha Bain, Graeme Henderson, Katherine Oliver, Rachel Spry and Simeon Truby.

MUSIC / *SONGS*

PART ONE:

1. Prologue
2. *Every Morning the Same*
3. Hopscotch
4. *Every Schoolday the Same*
5. Every Evening the Same
6. *Every Evening the Same* (reprise)
7. *The Argument*
8. *Put Him Back*
9. *Always the Same* (reprise)
10. Going Out
11. Balloon Theme
12. *Waiting for the Bus*
13. Running to School
14. *Frères Jacques* (trad.)
15. *Go Home*
16. *Please Can We Share Your Umbrella*
17. Back Home
18. At the Window
19. Next Morning
20. The Balloon Game
21. *Don't Get Lost*
22. *My Red Balloon*

PART TWO:

23. *Where's the Red Balloon Gone?*
24. The Classroom
25. Out of School
26. *The Games They Play*
27. *We Want the Red Balloon*
28. *Don't Get Lost* (reprise)
29. *The Market of Memories*
30. Clearing the Market
31. *We Saw You Talking to Him*
32. *Red and Blue*
33. *The Chase*
34. *I Will Miss You*
35. *The Revolt of the Balloons*
36. *Encore*

PART ONE

Prologue

Montmartre, Paris. 1956.

The light picks out a large helium-filled RED BALLOON floating, in front of a Paris skyscape. Enter the OPERATOR/PUPPETEER.

[M1]

He/she starts to manipulate the RED BALLOON. Slowly it is imbued with life and character.

(The OPERATOR/PUPPETEER should never reveal the RED BALLOON's character, and articulate its responses in their own face. Their focus should always be on the RED BALLOON.)

As the RED BALLOON dances and takes flight, the sky fills with a thousand stars.

Scene One

[M2]

A place where a number of streets converge. Gaslamps glow in the dark. One brighter than all the rest. Night to day. Dawn. A cat miaows as an old tin falls from a bin and rattles on the cobbles. Street sounds build as day breaks. The PEOPLE OF PARIS, starting with the LAMPLIGHTER extinguishing the lamps and an OLD WOMAN with a basket of fresh bread, appear and disappear, walking individually or in groups in the same and in different directions. The tune of the first song, 'Every Morning the Same', is clearly discernible and the movement of the crowd has quickened to a rush-hour pace, when PASCAL enters, and merges with them. The action stops, abruptly.

PASCAL

It's always the same,
Every morning, the same.

ALL

It's always the same,
Every morning, the same.

The action starts again.

MEN/WOMEN

We're rushing to be there on time.

CARETAKER

I'm cleaning the steps.

BOY

I'm polishing shoes.

WOMEN

We're hanging the clothes on the line.

ALL

It's always the same,
Every morning, the same.

POSTMAN

I'm pushing the post through your door.

TEACHER/HEAD/CHILDREN

We're going to school.

NEWSBOY

I'm selling the news.

SHOPKEEPER

I'm opening up the stall.

PASCAL

It's always the same –

ALL

Every morning, the same.

The CROWD collect newspapers from the NEWSBOY.

ALL

Have you read, have you read, have you read,
  have you read?
Have you heard, have you heard, have you
  heard what was said?
Have you seen, have you seen, have you seen,
  have you seen?
Have you thought, have you thought what it
  means?

MAN

It's written here in black and white!

CARETAKER

A picture too, to prove it's true!

TEACHER/HEAD

We have to know what's going on!

TEACHER

Who's in the right, who's in the wrong.

ALL

The price of peace, the cost of war;
Who won the race; the final score –

WOMAN

The stories that matter to me, and to you,
Are the dreams that we dream that come
  true.

ALL

To find that fortune, that place, that time,
When you make me your friend and I make
  you mine.

*The CROWD bustles. They wave, hail taxis, check their watches,
tie their laces, fold their papers, extinguish cigarettes, etc.*

PASCAL

Every hour of their day taken care of,
Every minute they've something to do.

ALL

We haven't the time, the will or the way –
Today is our busiest day.

The CROWD separates to reveal the GIRL.

PASCAL

I could be your friend, if you could be mine –
Please can you spare me your time?

ALL

We haven't the time, the will or the way
To stop what we're doing today.

The CROWD disappears.

PASCAL: Hello? My name's Pascal. Who are you? What's
your name? I'm called Pascal Lamorisse. Do you know
how to play hopscotch?

[M3]

*PASCAL draws a hopscotch court on the cobbles, and starts to
play. It doesn't take long before he throws his stone into the
wrong square.*

Your turn. You'll need a stone. Make sure you throw it in
the right square.

*The GIRL doesn't have a stone. She can't find one. PASCAL
offers her his.*

Here you are.

*The shrill sound of a TEACHER's whistle. Enter
SCHOOLCHILDREN and the TEACHER. PASCAL and
the GIRL join their peers. They establish a classroom. The
CHILDREN sit in pairs, in rows.*

[M4]

ALL

Always the same,
Every schoolday the same –
At school every day,
Where we rest work and play.

TEACHER

I teach them to see their minds grow.

GIRLS

We're learning to count.

BOYS

We're learning to read.

TEACHER

I'm teaching them all they should know.

ALL

It's always the same,
After school, it's the same.

The TEACHER blows her whistle.

TEACHER: Class dismissed.

The class disbands. The BOYS and GIRLS separate and hide.

CHILD 1: Pascal!

PASCAL stops and looks in the direction of the voice. Then from a different direction –

CHILD 3: Pascal!

And a different direction, again –

CHILD 4: Pascal!

PASCAL turns in response to each voice, and as he does so CHILD 1 and CHILD 2 rush at him, from behind. They push PASCAL and grab his satchel.

PASCAL: That's mine!

PASCAL attempts to retrieve his satchel from CHILD 1 as CHILD 2 rubs out the hopscotch court. More CHILDREN emerge from their hiding places. They throw PASCAL's satchel between them.

PASCAL: Give it back! That's mine!

CHILD 1: (*Throwing the satchel to another CHILD.*) Here, catch!

CHILD 3: Can't catch! Catch this!

PASCAL: (*Held back as he grabs for his satchel.*) Leave me alone!

CHILDREN: Can't catch! Can't catch!

CHILD 4 empties the contents of the satchel on the cobblestones.

CHILD 1: Catch!

CHILD 2: Catch!

CHILD 2 has found PASCAL's fountain pen, and threatens to break the nib on the stones.

PASCAL: Give it back!

CHILD 4: Dare you!

PASCAL: That's mine. Give it back! That's my best pen. Give it back or I'll tell!

The GIRL leaves.

PASCAL: Give it back. That's my new pen. That's my best pen! If you break the nib I'll tell. Don't break it. I'll never be your friend.

DON'T BREAK IT!

The CHILDREN stare in silence as CHILD 2 bends the nib on the cobbles – backwards and forwards until it breaks. CHILD 2 leaves the broken pen for PASCAL to pick up.

You've broken my pen.

CHILD 3: Pascal!

CHILD 4: Pascal!

The CHILDREN have PASCAL's exercise book. They hold it between them, threatening to tear it.

PASCAL: Don't tear it.

As PASCAL attempts to grab his book, one CHILD lets go. The CHILDREN turn their backs on PASCAL and it is unclear who has got the book. PASCAL picks the wrong person. Once. Twice. CHILD 5 reveals the book, and pretends to tear it. Much to the amusement of the other CHILDREN.

No. No, don't tear it. Please. That's my homework book. Don't tear it. That's my homework.

PASCAL rushes to CHILD 5 and jumps for his book. He has it, but CHILD 5 won't let go. The book is torn in two.

NO!

The CHILDREN laugh, as CHILD 5 tears the exercise book into small pieces, and scatters them over PASCAL.

The CHILDREN disperse. In silence PASCAL starts to pick up the remains of his homework book. Enter the GIRL, who dares to pick up one piece of paper and hand it to PASCAL before running away.

[M5]

It starts to rain.

As the PEOPLE OF PARIS drift home, night falls. A TRAMP searches the gutters and bins. The LAMPLIGHTER lights the lamps. A KITTEN miaows. PASCAL continues to gather the remains of his book, until he is distracted by a kitten miaowing, and goes off in search of it.

ALL

It's always the same,
Every evening, the same.

MAN

I'm taking my work home with me.

SHOPKEEPER

I'm counting the stock.

CARETAKER

I'm drawing the locks.

WOMAN

I'm bathing my tired baby.

ALL

It's always the same,
Every evening, the same.

PASCAL: (*To a TRAMP.*) You haven't lost a cat, have you?

TRAMP: (*No answer.*)

PASCAL: (*To TRAMP.*) Excuse me, but you haven't lost a cat, have you?

LAMPLIGHTER: You lost a cat?

PASCAL: No. Have you?

LAMPLIGHTER: What?

PASCAL: Lost a cat?

LAMPLIGHTER: Have *I* lost a cat?

PASCAL: Yes.

LAMPLIGHTER: No.

PASCAL disappears in search of the cat.

(*To TRAMP.*) There's plenty of strays around here.

PASCAL: (*Off.*) Kitty. Miaow! Kitty, kitty!

TRAMP: (*To LAMPLIGHTER.*) Evening.

PASCAL returns with the KITTEN.

PASCAL: It doesn't like the rain.

TRAMP: My cat didn't like the rain.

PASCAL: This isn't a cat, this is a kitten.

TRAMP: My cat was a kitten –

PASCAL: Is this yours?

TRAMP: Once. Once upon a time, I had a kitten for a cat.
What a cat! A proud tortoiseshell cat. Followed me
everywhere. Tail in the air. When I sat. She sat. Sat
on my lap. She purred. Prrr...I used to call her my
Purr Puss.

TWO NUNS pass by.

PASCAL: Excuse me, but you haven't lost a kitten have
you?

NUNS: Are you lost, child?

PASCAL: No.

NUNS: Good night.

They leave.

LAMPLIGHTER: Do you want that cat?

PASCAL: (*No answer.*)

*PASCAL empties his satchel, puts the kitten inside and tries
to keep his books dry by stuffing them under his jersey.*

25

LAMPLIGHTER: (*Referring to the TRAMP.*) There are plenty of strays around here. Be glad of a home. Be very glad of a good home...a stray (*Catching the TRAMP looking at him.*)...a stray *cat*.

PASCAL: Do you light the lamp every day?

LAMPLIGHTER: Every night. Every day, I put it out. Good night.

PASCAL: Good night.

LAMPLIGHTER: Night.

PASCAL: (*To KITTEN.*) Do you like sardines?

TRAMP: They're my favourite.

PASCAL: I wasn't talking to you.

TRAMP: Good night.

PASCAL: Good night.

Would you like a saucer of milk?

PASCAL rushes home, through a tired CROWD.

[M6]

ALL

It's always the same,
Every evening, the same.
We're busy, we've too much to do –
Too busy to stop
To just say hello,
To take any notice of you.

Scene Two

[M7]

Morning. PASCAL's home. A small flat, modestly decorated. MAMAN and PAPA have had breakfast. PAPA is reading the newspaper;

MAMAN is agitated as PASCAL isn't ready for school. PASCAL, who looks as though he has dressed in a hurry, hasn't yet had any breakfast. He is preoccupied trying to coax HERCULE (for that is what he has called his kitten), out from under the sideboard. HERCULE is miaowing, pitifully.

MAMAN

More coffee.

MAMAN pours PAPA another cup of coffee.

PAPA

Good morning, Pascal.

PASCAL: Hercule –

MAMAN

Say good morning to Papa, Pascal.

PAPA

Up all night playing with that cat –

PASCAL: No, Papa.

MAMAN

Say good morning to Papa, Pascal.

PASCAL: Good morning, Papa.

MAMAN

You look tired.

PASCAL: Hercule is stuck under the sofa.

MAMAN

Get ready for school or the cat goes back.

PASCAL: Papa said he could stay –

MAMAN

It's not allowed.

                    PAPA

    That was last night.

PASCAL: But Papa said –

                    PAPA

    If it's allowed.

PASCAL: You said you'd ask.

                    PAPA

    Are your shoes clean?

                    MAMAN

    If you eat your breakfast.

PASCAL: You will ask, won't you, Papa?

                    PAPA

    If there's time –

PASCAL: You promised –

                    PAPA

    That was yesterday.

PASCAL: Please, Papa!

                    PAPA

    It was your mother's fault.

                    MAMAN

    We had to get him to bed.

PASCAL: Maman, he promised.

                    PAPA

    We can't afford it.

                    MAMAN

    Come and eat your breakfast.

PAPA

I may be out of a job!

PASCAL: He won't cost anything. He can eat my food.

PAPA

What's that smell?

PASCAL: I'm not going to school.

MAMAN

Yes you are!

PAPA

Can't you smell it?

PASCAL: It's not fair on Hercule.

MAMAN

It's not fair on me, Pascal.
Just look at the state of you!
We'll never be ready on time.

PAPA

Are you telling me you can't smell anything?

MAMAN

I'm too busy.

PAPA

I'm feeling sick.

MAMAN

There's a bucket under the sink –

PASCAL: He won't come out.

PAPA

The smell's unbearable!

MAMAN

There's a newspaper on the table,

And a mop by the door!

PAPA

The cat's pooed on the carpet.

MAMAN

There's plenty of hot water in the kettle,
And some disinfectant under the sink.
Come on, Pascal!

PASCAL: He's so frightened, he's shaking like a leaf!

PAPA

The cat's pooed on the new carpet!

PASCAL: It's not his fault.

PAPA

It's yours, get rid of it!

PASCAL: He couldn't help it. How would you like it –

PAPA

I don't like it.

PASCAL: You promised you'd ask.

PAPA

How else were we going to get you to bed?
It was half past eleven and –
(*Turning on MAMAN.*) This is all your fault,
this is!

HERCULE miaows.

MAMAN

I never said he could keep it here.
You said –

PAPA

I never said he could keep it here.

                    MAMAN

You said –

                     PAPA

I know the rules and regulations in this flat!

                    MAMAN

He said, you said,
If he was good, he could –

                     PAPA

It doesn't matter what I said,
But I didn't say anything of the sort.

                    MAMAN

You don't know what you said.
He said, you said, if he was good he could –

                     PAPA

I never said that!

                    MAMAN

You did.

                     PAPA

When did I say that?

                    MAMAN

Last night!

                     PAPA

Well, he can't have heard what I said then.

                    MAMAN

Every word –

                     PAPA

He misheard.

                    MAMAN

All that you said he heard –

PAPA

Well, what did I say?

MAMAN

You said –

PAPA

Every word –

MAMAN

All he said –

PAPA

You can't remember a word!

PASCAL: Maman, Hercule is stuck!

MAMAN

You said we should –

PAPA

We shouldn't.

MAMAN

You said we could –

PAPA

How can we?

MAMAN

You never listen to me!

PAPA

To me!

MAMAN

You never listen to me!

PASCAL: Hercule is stuck under here.

PAPA

It doesn't matter.

MAMAN

It does.

PAPA

Look, I don't mind what –

MAMAN

I do!

PAPA

Bear it in mind how I feel –

MAMAN

I feel it too!

They shake their heads.

PAPA/MAMAN

So we do –
We share the same point of view.

PAPA: Let Pascal clear it up. It's his cat.

PASCAL: Can I keep it then?

MAMAN/PAPA: No!

PASCAL: I'm not helping then.

MAMAN: (*Holding out a bucket and dustpan to PAPA.*) Hold this.

PAPA: (*Dropping the dustpan and bucket to put on his coat and hat.*) I must go. I'm going to be late.

MAMAN: (*Offering the bucket to PASCAL.*) Pascal?

PASCAL: No, Maman, the smell makes me feel funny.

MAMAN: Sit down and eat your breakfast or you go to school without anything.

PASCAL perches on the edge of his seat, gobbles his food and slurps his drink.

MAMAN: Pascal!

PAPA: Where's my case? Has that cat been playing with my case?

MAMAN hands him his case.

(*Hissing aggressively at HERCULE.*) Ssss! (*Slapping his pockets.*) Keys? Keys? Have you two been playing with my keys?

MAMAN: In the door.

PAPA finds his keys.

PAPA: (*Hissing at HERCULE.*) Ssss!

PAPA: Hat? Where's my hat? Has that cat been sleeping in my hat?

PASCAL: You're wearing it.

PAPA: (*Barks at HERCULE.*) Woof! Woof! Woof!

MAMAN: Goodbye, darling.

PAPA: Goodbye.

MAMAN/PAPA: (*They kiss.*) Goodbye.

PAPA: Make sure you get rid of that cat.

PASCAL: But Papa you promised.

PAPA: It pooed on the carpet. That cat –

MAMAN: (*Shooing PAPA out of the door.*) Go on! You're late. Later than late. Go! Go! Go on! Get out!

PAPA leaves, and returns immediately.

PAPA: Get rid of it.

PAPA leaves. Silence, while MAMAN cleans the carpet and PASCAL tries to rescue HERCULE.

PASCAL: Will you ask, Maman?

MAMAN: You know the rules.

PASCAL: But he's so small.

MAMAN: It makes no difference.

PASCAL: We could hide him in my room and nobody would know.

MAMAN: What about the smell? Living in a flat. It's not fair on a cat.

PASCAL: It's not fair on me. I've got no one to play with.

[M8]

MAMAN brushes PASCAL's hair and straightens his clothes.

MAMAN

You've no brothers and sisters
But you're not alone.
You've got plenty of toys
To play on your own.

PASCAL

I'll enjoy my toys more
If Hercule can stay.
He'll be quiet and tidy,
He'll keep out of your way.

MAMAN

Put him back where you found him,
He'll be happier there.
Living here on his own,
It's very unfair.

You know how much we love you –

PASCAL

You only pretend.

MAMAN

All that we have, we give you –

PASCAL

But I haven't a friend.

MAMAN

Put him back where you found him –

PASCAL

Other children have pets –

MAMAN

He'll be happier there –

PASCAL

Other children do –

MAMAN

Living here on his own –

PASCAL

Other parents don't mind –

MAMAN

Is very unfair.

PASCAL

So why must you?

MAMAN	PASCAL
What some parents do,	You don't understand –
That's their affair.	He's got nowhere to go.
It's got nothing to do	He wants to stay here –
With how we live here.	He told me, I know!

Put him back where you
      found him,
It's never too late.
They say cats have nine lives,
We'll leave this one to fate.

PASCAL

You don't understand, Maman –

MAMAN

I think I do.
You don't understand, Pascal –

PASCAL

Maman, do you?
Please, Maman –

MAMAN

No, Pascal.

PASCAL: Please, please, please!

MAMAN

Not even for you.

PASCAL collects a cardboard box to carry HERCULE back to the street, sulkily.

MAMAN: Did you do your homework?

PASCAL: Yes, Maman.

MAMAN: Let me see.

Pause.

MAMAN: Pascal, you did do your homework last night, didn't you? Let me see your book.

PASCAL: We weren't given any.

MAMAN: You've always got homework. What do you mean you weren't given any? Where's your book?

What were you supposed to do? Let me see your book. (*Picking up his satchel, she looks inside.*) Pascal!

PASCAL: (*No answer.*)

MAMAN: What've you been doing?

PASCAL: It was an accident. It was raining, and I was running to get home, and I dropped my book, and it fell open, and the page with my homework on fell in a puddle, and all the ink ran, and then I tore out the page because I didn't want to ruin the whole book.

MAMAN: Are you telling me the truth?

PASCAL: I promise you, it's true.

MAMAN pulls out scraps of exercise book, from PASCAL's satchel.

MAMAN: Don't lie to me, Pascal.

PASCAL: And I dropped my pen.

MAMAN: Your new pen?

PASCAL: Yes, Maman. And the nib broke.

MAMAN: Pascal, that was a new pen. Very expensive.

PASCAL: I couldn't help it, Maman. Everything fell out of my satchel. I had to protect Hercule from the rain. Cats don't like water, do they? I had to put him in my satchel, and then I wanted to keep my books dry, so I put them under my jersey. But they wouldn't stay and they kept falling out.

MAMAN: Why do you do this to me? You're so late. Here, you'd better borrow my pen. Your satchel's for carrying books. Nothing else. No cats, no dogs. Books, Pascal. Put Hercule back where you found him, and throw away that box. Now go. Quick, or you'll be late for school.

PASCAL puts HERCULE into the box, and leaves.

PASCAL: Come on, Hercule, or we'll be late. Say goodbye.

MAMAN: Goodbye, Pascal.

PASCAL: Hercule, say 'thank you'. Miaow!

[M9]

PASSERS-BY pass PASCAL, taking no notice.

PASSERS-BY

Every hour of the day taken care of,
Every minute we've something to do.
We haven't the time, the will or the way –
It's always our busiest day.

Scene Three

Morning. The street. A TRAMP is asleep beside an old dustbin. The RED BALLOON descends from the sky above Paris and gets itself caught on the tallest lamppost. The TRAMP stirs. Enter PASCAL with HERCULE still in the cardboard box.

TRAMP: What have you got for me?

PASCAL: Nothing.

TRAMP: I've got nothing. What else?

PASCAL: Nothing else.

TRAMP: What's in that box then?

PASCAL: The kitten.

TRAMP: Purr Puss?

PASCAL: Hercule.

TRAMP: (*Looking at the cat.*) She looks younger than I remember...

PASCAL: He's one day older.

TRAMP: And smaller...

PASCAL: You don't remember him, do you? Do you remember me?

TRAMP: Yesterday, I remember –

PASCAL: He was crying in the rain.

TRAMP: You were crying in the rain.

PASCAL: Cats don't like the rain.

TRAMP: Neither do I.

PASCAL: I'm not allowed to keep Hercule, because I live in a flat. And Maman and Papa don't like cats, though they pretend they do. Papa says he'll ask the concierge if I can keep Hercule, but he'll forget. He always does. And Maman said it's not fair. Can you look after him for me? He's never a nuisance. He likes playing all the time. I'll bring you my scraps for him to eat. He doesn't eat much, he's got a very small stomach. Please? Just until Maman and Papa stop arguing, and Papa stops worrying about how much money he hasn't got, and he remembers to ask the concierge to change the rules.

TRAMP: (*Taking the box. To HERCULE.*) Let's see how strong you are.

PASCAL: Don't lose him, will you?

TRAMP: (*Putting his hand into the box.*) Oiw!

PASCAL: Be careful.

TRAMP: Tiger.

PASCAL: See you soon, Hercule. Raggedy will look after you.

[M10]

The TRAMP and PASCAL go their separate ways.

[M11]

PASCAL sees the RED BALLOON. He looks around to see if it belongs to anyone. Nobody there. He moves towards the lamppost. He is just about to start climbing when TWO PEOPLE cross the playing area, in one direction – too busy to stop, although one notices the RED BALLOON, momentarily. The music stops. An OLD MAN crosses from another direction. He stops as though he has heard something. Sees the RED BALLOON. Shakes his head and moves on.

PASCAL: I found you. You're mine.

The music continues, as PASCAL starts to climb the lamppost. A PERSON enters, and the music stops. PASCAL stops climbing. The PERSON (he/she) notices PASCAL, and the RED BALLOON. The PERSON points to the RED BALLOON. PASCAL nods. The PERSON moves on. The music continues as PASCAL climbs.

PASCAL: Finders keepers.

A LOST MAN enters. PASCAL stops climbing. The music stops. The LOST MAN consults a map. Rapidly sorts out his right from his left and runs away. The music continues as PASCAL climbs.

PASCAL: That man hasn't lost this balloon. But if I asked him, he'd say he had.

A WOMAN passes with a pram. The baby inside is crying. PASCAL stops again, and so does the music. The WOMAN turns her pram and points out the RED BALLOON to the baby. The baby stops crying. The WOMAN continues on her way. The music continues as PASCAL reaches the top of the lamppost.

PASCAL: That baby's too small for this balloon.

Enter TWO GIRLS. One chasing the other. The music stops. PASCAL freezes. The GIRL leaves her friend to run on when she sees PASCAL. She stares at him.

PASCAL: It's rude to stare.

PASCAL unties the balloon and brings it down safely, holding the string between his teeth.

This yours?

GIRL: I think so.

PASCAL: Prove it.

The GIRL rushes off.

PASCAL: I must catch the bus or I'll be late for school.

[M12]

Scene Four

A line of five people gather to form a bus queue. PERSON 1, who just beats PERSON 2 to the front of the queue, is a smart business type. PERSON 2 is laden down with heavy shopping bags. PERSON 3 is perhaps the most impatient of all those in the queue. He/she looks at his/her watch every couple of seconds, while trying to read the newspaper. PERSONS 4 and 5 are young and prone to falling in love with strangers.

PERSONS 2, 3, 4 & 5

I'll stand behind you –

PERSON 1

In an orderly queue.

PERSON 3

We must wait for the bus to come.

ALL

And if our eyes meet
When we shuffle our feet –

PERSON 4 (*To PERSON 5.*)

I'll bow, admiring the view.

ALL

Waiting, waiting,
Waiting for the bus to come.
We'll grow old waiting,
Waiting for the bus to come.

PERSON 3

I cannot concentrate,
While I have to wait.

PERSON 2

I've never known this bus on time.

PERSON 4

They never say why –

PERSON 5

Though they tell you they try –

ALL

But rush hour means the bus runs late.

Waiting, waiting,
Waiting for the bus to come.
We'll grow old waiting,
Waiting for the bus to come.

Enter PASCAL and the RED BALLOON. They join the back of the queue. It is either the will of the RED BALLOON or the wind that blows it between PERSONS 4 & 5 just at the point when they dare to kiss each other; that places the RED BALLOON under PERSON 3's open newspaper and starts to lift that paper up up and away; that bounces the balloon on PERSON 2's bottom, while he/she is checking the contents of one of his/her bags. PERSON 2 believes it to be PERSON 1 taking advantage of the situation, and promptly hits him. PERSON 1 smiles to apologise, and removes his hat. The RED BALLOON pummels his head until his knees buckle.

PASCAL and the RED BALLOON are now at the front of the queue, much to the annoyance of the other travellers.

ALL

We'll have to be stern.
Young man, will you learn –

PERSON 1

And get to the back of the queue!

PERSONS 4 & 5

The bus is due soon –

ALL

Better lose that balloon.

Wait over there, wait your turn.
Waiting, waiting,
Waiting for the bus to come.
We'll grow old waiting,
Waiting for the bus.

Now we're late,
We're very late,
We can't afford the time to wait!
We'll grow old waiting,
Waiting for the bus.

The bus is driven on. (The size and speed of the bus is defined by the actors playing the PASSENGERS, the DRIVER, and the BUS CONDUCTOR.) As the bus approaches the bus stop, PERSONS 4 & 5 who have been holding back PASCAL and the RED BALLOON let go. The RED BALLOON pulls PASCAL into the back of the queue with such force that all in the queue bump each other, knocking over PERSON 1. They trample over PERSON 1 until he is at the back of the queue. In order to retrieve his hat, which he has dropped where he was standing, he scrambles through the legs of the queue to find himself at the front just as the bus comes to a stop. The queue breaks up as everybody pushes and shoves to be the first on the bus.

BUS CONDUCTOR

There's no need to push,
You'll avoid the great crush
If you form an orderly queue.
Don't push, or you'll fall,
There's room for you all –
You'll get nowhere fast in a rush.

ALL except PASCAL and the RED BALLOON get on to the bus.

BUS CONDUCTOR: We're full.

PASCAL: But I'll be late.

BUS CONDUCTOR: Sorry.

PASSENGERS

Tut tut! Tut tut!

PASCAL: I'm very small.

BUS CONDUCTOR: I'm sorry.

PASCAL: But I catch this bus to school every day.

BUS CONDUCTOR: Not with that, you don't.

PASCAL: What?

BUS CONDUCTOR: That balloon.

PASCAL: This is my balloon.

BUS CONDUCTOR: I don't care whose it is. It's not allowed on the bus.

No dogs, no cats
And no large parcels,
And definitely –

45

PASSENGERS
Definitely, definitely,
No gas-filled
red balloons.

Nothing in here
Must interfere
With passengers on
     the bus.

BUS CONDUCTOR

Nothing in here   People with pets,
Must interfere   They all have to walk,
With passengers on Take packages by taxi.
     the bus.

ALL

Stay out there,
Don't interfere
With us, we're on the bus.

PASSENGERS   BUS CONDUCTOR

Nothing in here   Let it loose,
Must interfere   Let your balloon go
With passengers on Before you get on to
     the bus.   the bus.

PASCAL: We won't get in the way, I promise.

ALL

Waiting, waiting,
Waiting for the bus to leave.
We'll grow old waiting,
Waiting for the bus.

The BUS CONDUCTOR rings the bell, and the bus drives away.

PASCAL: I must run as fast as I can, or I'll be late
   for school.

[M13]

PASCAL runs with the RED BALLOON to school, dodging the traffic and the people in the street.

Scene Five

PASCAL arrives in the school courtyard. In front of the classroom door. The caretaker, ALBERT, is sweeping/mopping out the yard. Behind the classroom door PASCAL's class are learning 'Frère Jacques or another suitable song.

[M14]

PASCAL creeps unnoticed through the classroom door, but the RED BALLOON gets trapped the wrong side of the door. The singing stops. ALBERT notices the RED BALLOON and walks towards it. The singing starts again. The door opens and PASCAL comes out to retrieve his balloon. He takes it inside and the singing grinds to a halt. PASCAL rushes out. The singing starts up again. Pascal stands there holding the RED BALLOON as it bobs up and down to look through glass panels in the top half of the classroom door.

CHILDREN

Frère Jacques, Frère Jacques
Dormez-vous, dormez-vous ?
Sonnez les matines
Sonnez les matines
Din, din, don!
Din, din, don!

(Repeated as many times as is necessary.)

ALBERT: Good afternoon, Pascal.

PASCAL: Good morning, Albert.

ALBERT: You're late.

PASCAL: I've never been late before.

ALBERT: You're very, very late.

PASCAL: The bus conductor wouldn't let me on the bus. He said my balloon would get in the way.

ALBERT: Rules and regulations.

PASCAL: So I ran here, as fast as I could.

ALBERT: The first time you're late, it doesn't matter, but the second time, they don't forget the first, and then Mademoiselle Elaine will tell your mother and father.

Pause.

ALBERT: That's a big balloon.

PASCAL: It's mine.

ALBERT: As big as the moon.

PASCAL: It's just an ordinary balloon.

ALBERT: Where did you get it?

PASCAL: It's mine.

ALBERT plays with the RED BALLOON, poking it with his broom. The RED BALLOON takes exception to this and biffs ALBERT on the head. ALBERT enjoys this, and head-butts the RED BALLOON back for fun.

PASCAL: Be careful! It'll burst.

ELAINE: (*In the classroom.*) Pascal!

PASCAL: You'll burst it. It was lost in the wind, and it got stuck on a lamppost. It tied itself up, and I climbed up the lamppost and I rescued it, all by myself.

ALBERT: Someone's lost a beautiful balloon.

ELAINE: (*In the classroom.*) Pascal!

PASCAL: I'm coming, Mlle Elaine. No one lost it.

ALBERT: You can't take that balloon in there.

PASCAL: Finders keepers.

ALBERT: They'll all want to play with it. I'll look after it for you.

PASCAL: No.

ALBERT: I'll look after it.

ELAINE: (*In the classroom.*) Pascal, you're late!

PASCAL: I've never been late before, Mlle Elaine.

ALBERT: I'll lock it in the shed. It'll be perfectly safe. Nobody goes in there.

PASCAL: You'll burst it.

ALBERT: Trust me.

PASCAL: You mustn't play with it.

ALBERT: I've got work to do.

ELAINE: Pascal!

ALBERT: You'll remember to collect it before you go home.

PASCAL: Coming, Mlle Elaine. I'm just tying my shoelaces.

ELAINE: (*Emerging from the classroom.*) Pascal!

PASCAL gives ALBERT the RED BALLOON and slips back into the classroom. The RED BALLOON tries to follow and pulls ALBERT into ELAINE. ALBERT is delighted to have the opportunity to hold ELAINE, but he wouldn't want her to get the wrong impression.

ELAINE: What's going on?

ALBERT: Sorry, sorry, sorry.

ELAINE: Albert!

ALBERT: The stone is wet. Be careful not to slip.

As ALBERT tries to demonstrate how slippery the stones are, the RED BALLOON pulls him backwards.

Oooh!

ALBERT, now flat on his back, has his arm tugged backwards and forwards, as the RED BALLOON tries to break free and join PASCAL in the classroom.

There, you see!

ELAINE: The stone is perfectly dry.

ALBERT: Then my shoes are wet.

ELAINE: Where did you get that balloon?

ALBERT: I'm looking after it for a friend, Mademoiselle Elaine.

PASCAL comes out of the classroom, and the RED BALLOON is still.

PASCAL: It's mine.

ELAINE: The rule is, you don't bring toys to school, Pascal.

PASCAL: Yes, Mlle Elaine.

ALBERT: I'll look after it.

PASCAL: He'll burst it, Mlle Elaine.

ELAINE: Get in there.

PASCAL: But what about my balloon?

ELAINE: You're late.

PASCAL: I've never been late before.

ELAINE ushers Pascal into the classroom. Again the RED BALLOON tries to follow, and sends ALBERT crashing into the classroom door. ALBERT is used as a human battering ram, but to no avail: no one will open the door to the RED BALLOON. Defeated, bruised and unable to pull the RED BALLOON away from the door, ALBERT decides to tie it to the handle. This he does, and continues sweeping the yard. It isn't very long before he realises that the RED BALLOON, bobbing up and down in front of the windows in the door, is causing chaos in the class. Uproar. ELAINE is at the window, blowing her whistle and signalling to ALBERT to stop the RED BALLOON. ALBERT has a brainwave. He takes off his overalls and smothers the RED BALLOON. The RED BALLOON doesn't like being blindfolded, and behaves like a dazed rabbit in a poacher's bag, shifting from side to side, up and down under his overalls. ALBERT, however, is now able to control it and escorts the RED BALLOON to his shed, where he locks it up.

Scene Six

The whistle blows for the end of class.

[M15]

PASCAL rushes out of the classroom. He looks this way and that for ALBERT and the RED BALLOON. He tries ALBERT's shed, but the door is locked.

PASCAL: Albert! Albert! Albert!

There is no sign of ALBERT, as the other CHILDREN come out of the classroom.

ALBERT!

If anyone sees Albert, tell him I'm waiting for him.

CHILD 1: Where's your red balloon gone?

PASCAL: (*No answer.*)

CHILD 2: Must've blown away...

PASCAL: (*No answer.*)

CHILDREN: Maybe it burst.

PASCAL: No.

CHILD 4: Well, where is it then?

CHILDREN 5 & 6: Where is it?

PASCAL: (*No answer.*)

CHILD 2: I know where it is.

CHILDREN: Where?

PASCAL: No you don't.

CHILD 3: He knows where it is.

CHILD 2: Tell me.

CHILD 3: All of us.

GIRL: He's lost it.

CHILD 4: If you don't tell us –

CHILD 2: We'll never play with you.

CHILD 1: Never.

CHILD 3: We'll never play with you again.

CHILDREN: Never, never, never.

> *The CHILDREN start to bully PASCAL, brutally. The GIRL runs to tell ELAINE. ELAINE dashes out of the classroom with her umbrella – pulling the CHILDREN off PASCAL to protect him –*

ELAINE

That's enough, go home,
All of you, go home.
Leave Pascal alone.
Go home.

CHILDREN

We want to play with
The big red balloon!
If he brings it to school
He must share, that's the rule!
Where's the balloon,
The big red balloon?

Balloon, red balloon
We want the red balloon!
He's got to tell us,
He's hidden it away.
We'll make him tell us,
We'll force him to say.

Balloon, red balloon
Where is the red balloon?

ELAINE

All of you, go home.
Leave Pascal alone.
That's enough, go home.
Go home.

The CHILDREN start to leave. Some linger to protest their case. The GIRL stays to the last.

If you bring toys to school
You must share,
That's the rule.
If you've lost your balloon,
Not a moment too soon.

PASCAL

But you don't understand, Miss –

ELAINE

Yes I do.

PASCAL

Miss, you don't understand –

PASCAL moves to ALBERT's door.

My balloon's in there,
All alone in there,
Running out of air
On its own in there.

ELAINE: It's time to go home.

PASCAL: Where's Albert?

ELAINE: Go home, or you'll be late and your mother will
worry. (*Noticing the GIRL.*) And the same applies to you.

*Before she leaves, the GIRL picks up ELAINE's umbrella,
and hands it to her.*

PASCAL: But what about my balloon?

ELAINE: Tomorrow.

PASCAL: Yes, Mlle Elaine.

ELAINE: Don't be late.

PASCAL: No, Mlle Elaine.

*Enter ALBERT jangling a large ring of keys, oblivious to the
time of day.*

ALBERT: Good evening, Mademoiselle Elaine.

ELAINE: Good afternoon, Albert.

PASCAL: Where have you been?

ALBERT: (*To ELAINE.*) Working late?

ELAINE: Waiting for you!

ALBERT: (*Going down on one knee.*) You are the sunshine in
my life –

ELAINE: Don't be a fool.

ALBERT: Such a beautiful afternoon, and the clouds go and sweep the smile off the sun. Just like that.

PASCAL: I want my balloon back.

ALBERT: Lucky you brought your umbrella.

ELAINE: Albert, Pascal's balloon!

ALBERT: I might have known, my seaweed was damp.

PASCAL: Give me my balloon back. I'm late!

ELAINE: ALBERT, WOULD YOU PLEASE UNLOCK YOUR DOOR AND GIVE PASCAL'S BALLOON BACK!

ALBERT: I knew there was something. The business of the day swept it clean away. How could I forget?

PASCAL: You shouldn't have forgotten –

ELAINE: Pascal!

ALBERT: You don't understand, it's easy to forget when you're old. (*Looking at ELAINE, admiringly.*) But when you're young...Don't forget if you're late tomorrow, she won't have forgotten that you were late today.

PASCAL: It'll be running out of air!

ALBERT: I'll fetch it for you. It's been no trouble. No trouble at all.

ALBERT unlocks his door, and just manages to grab the RED BALLOON as it flies towards PASCAL. ALBERT loses his balance and ends up, winded, on the floor – still holding on to the RED BALLOON. PASCAL tries to wrench it free, but ALBERT's hand is set in a vice-like grip. The RED BALLOON tickles him, and is released into PASCAL's hands.

ELAINE: Tomorrow.

PASCAL: Yes, Mlle Elaine.

ELAINE: Don't be late.

PASCAL: No Mlle Elaine. But, I'm not allowed to take my balloon on the bus.

ELAINE: Leave it at home, there's a good boy.

ALBERT: (*Recovering.*) If I didn't think you'd never believe me, I'd tell you that balloon has a life of its own.

PASCAL: (*To ALBERT.*) Don't ever do that again.

ALBERT: What have I done now?

ELAINE: Say 'thank you, Albert' for looking after the red balloon.

ALBERT: (*Looking deep into ELAINE's eyes.*) Thank you.

PASCAL: Thank you Albert for looking after my red balloon.

PASCAL leaves with his RED BALLOON.

ALBERT: Mademoiselle Elaine?

ELAINE; Yes, Albert.

ALBERT: You don't know how often I've met you in my dreams.

ELAINE: (*Not wanting to pursue the subject.*) Yes, Albert.

ALBERT: And how I wish I didn't have to wake up at the moment when – Tell me you dream of me?

ELAINE: What?

ALBERT: That I star in your dreams as regularly as you star in mine. That we are both dreaming the same dream at the same time. In which case it needn't be a dream at all, need it, Mademoiselle Elaine?

ELAINE: Are you alright?

ALBERT: I'm dreaming.

ELAINE: What?

ALBERT: Kiss me!

A clap of thunder.

Have you never felt the pain of love, Mademoiselle? The boot in the stomach. The corkscrew in the heart? The wind?

ELAINE: (*Threatening to slap him.*) Try that again, and you'll feel nothing but the back of my hand!

Another clap of thunder. ELAINE puts up her umbrella and walks away. ALBERT trundles off in the opposite direction, defeated.

[M16]

Scene Seven

PASCAL walks the RED BALLOON home through the streets of Paris, in the rain. They meet PASSERS-BY, all adequately clothed for the weather, but some more inclined than others to share their umbrellas.

NEWSBOY rushes past with a newspaper on his head.

PASCAL meets two NUNS under one umbrella.

PASCAL

If you don't mind, and you're walking our way,
Please can we share your umbrella?

The two NUNS move away. Enter a BUSINESSMAN, with 'matters of consequence' on his mind.

If you don't mind, and you're walking our way,
Please can we share your umbrella?

BUSINESSMAN (*Retreating.*)

I'm sorry to say, I'm not walking your way.
I've a meeting at the Café Bella.

*BUSINESSMAN moves away and, like everybody in this
sequence (dance), will leave the playing area only to reappear
walking in a different direction. The scene is soon awash
with umbrellas. Enter a person in a great hurry, the
HURRIER.*

PASCAL

If you don't mind –

HURRIER

I most certainly do!

PASCAL

Please can we share your umbrella?

HURRIER

Your big red balloon is blocking my view.
I'm not walking round the town with you.

HURRIER scurries away. Enter the RELAXED MAN.

PASCAL

If you don't mind –

RELAXED MAN

And I'm walking your way,
Yes, you can share my umbrella.

ALL

See them dash from umbrella to umbrella,
Let the rain try and catch them if it can.
See them splash, see them skip, see them hop,
As they try to avoid every drop.

Listen to the rainfall,
Listen to the rain,

Every drop of rainfall,
Listen to the rain.

PASCAL tries another PASSER-BY.

PASCAL

If you don't mind –

PASSER-BY

And I'm walking your way,
Yes, you can share this umbrella.

Young man, I go this way –

PASCAL

– that way !

PASSER-BY

Go find another umbrella.

ALL

See them dash from umbrella to umbrella,
Let the rain try and catch them if it can.
See them splash, see them skip, see them hop,
As they try to avoid every drop.

Listen to the rainfall,
Listen to the rain,
Every drop of rainfall,
Listen to the rain.

No, you can't share this umbrella,
No, we're not walking your way.
If you haven't a coat for this weather,
Why should we bother with you?

An OLD MAN passes by.

PASCAL

If you don't mind,
And you're walking our way,
Please can we share your umbrella?

OLD MAN

Yes, you can share my umbrella,
But will you both fit under here?

PASCAL

Yes, there is plenty of room
If I stand underneath my balloon.

OLD MAN

Now I'm old, no one bothers with me –
My life is seen as history.
Before the war, I remember when
We skated the frozen Seine.

PASCAL

When I grow up, guess what I'm going to be:
The first man to walk on the moon.
I'm going to fly in a rocket past the stars
And I'm going to take my big red balloon.

ALL

They walked home underneath that umbrella,
Talking and laughing all the way.
See them hop, see them jump, see them run,
As they dance in the rain,
Dance in the rain,
Dance in the rain,
Having fun.

PASCAL: This is home. This is where I live.

[M17]

They separate.

Scene Eight

The flat. MAMAN is on the telephone.

MAMAN: No, I'm not in love. I've never been in love,
Albert. Well, once. Briefly. There's someone coming.

The sound of PASCAL entering the flat. MAMAN drops the receiver.

Is that you, Pascal?

Pascal?

PASCAL enters. MAMAN goes to give him a big hug.

MAMAN: Where've you been? You're all wet.

PASCAL: It's raining. But we managed to share umbrellas most of the way.

MAMAN: Where've you been? I've been so worried. Worried sick. Why didn't you take the bus? You had your fare, didn't you? I was so worried, and your father, and the neighbours and their neighbours. And when I eventually get through to the school to try and find out what's been happening I speak to that idiot Albert who tells me you're walking home in this weather. You'll catch your death.

MAMAN notices she hasn't put back the receiver. Putting it back.

This is all your fault, this is.

PASCAL: I'm sorry.

MAMAN: I thought something terrible had happened.

PASCAL: Maman, I couldn't help it.

MAMAN: What do you mean, you couldn't help it? I'm angry with you, Pascal. Very angry.

MAMAN slaps PASCAL.

PASCAL: Oiwww! The bus conductor wouldn't let me on the bus with the balloon.

MAMAN: Where did you get that balloon?

PASCAL: I rescued it. It was caught on a lamppost, and I climbed up –

MAMAN: Give me that balloon.

PASCAL: Why, Maman?

MAMAN: When did you find this balloon?

PASCAL: This morning.

MAMAN: Where did you find it?

PASCAL: It was lost.

MAMAN: How much did you spend?

PASCAL: I found it.

MAMAN: Are you telling me the truth?

PASCAL: (*Pulling his bus fare out of his pocket.*) Yes, Maman.

MAMAN: You were late home because of this balloon?

PASCAL: Yes, Maman.

MAMAN: Then I shall put it back where you found it.

MAMAN grabs the RED BALLOON and throws it out of the window.

PASCAL: No, Maman, no, Maman. That's my balloon. MAMAN!

MAMAN: There. Now, sit down and do your homework while I finish the supper.

PASCAL: It's not fair.

MAMAN: Have you brought your homework home with you?

PASCAL: Yes, Maman. But it's not fair.

MAMAN: Be fair to me, Pascal. I was worried sick.

PASCAL: I've got a lot of homework.

MAMAN goes into the kitchen.

MAMAN: Now look what you've made me do. I've burnt
the sardines.

PASCAL: That's not my fault.

MAMAN: They're your favourite.

PASCAL: No they're not.

MAMAN: You'll have to make do with bread and jam.

PASCAL: I'm not hungry.

*Pascal, despondent, sits at the table and takes out his
homework.*

[M18]

*Very, very quietly, Pascal gets up from his chair and creeps
over to the window. He pulls back the curtains. The RED
BALLOON has stayed outside the window. They look at
each other through the glass. The RED BALLOON bounces
itself on the window pane. PASCAL opens the window, and
the RED BALLOON flies in. It explores the room.*

MAMAN: Pascal!

PASCAL: What, Maman?

MAMAN: What are you doing?

PASCAL: Just doing my homework. (*To the RED
BALLOON.*) Hide. (*Lifting up the tablecloth.*) Hide under
here...until I've finished my reading...and my bread and
jam. I won't be long, and then we can play.

The RED BALLOON hides under the table.

MAMAN: (*Off.*) Pascal?

PASCAL: Yes, Maman, I'm very busy.

MAMAN: Don't you ever do that again.

PASCAL: No, Maman.

PASCAL closes the window and curtains as MAMAN enters.

MAMAN: What are you doing?

PASCAL: Just closing the curtains, because it's so late.

PASCAL returns to the table, and his satchel.

MAMAN: And we know whose fault that is, don't we? Where's my pen?

PASCAL: (*Holding up her pen.*) Here, Maman.

MAMAN: Don't ever do that again.

Scene Nine

[M19]

The next day. Morning. PASCAL lets the RED BALLOON out of the window, and gets ready for school, quickly.

MAMAN: Pascal, don't forget –

PASCAL: No, Maman.

PASCAL rushes out of the flat and finds himself in the street outside. He looks up at the window, where the RED BALLOON is waiting for him.

PASCAL: Balloon, Red Balloon!

[M20]

The RED BALLOON glides down, to meet PASCAL. He grabs hold of it, and acknowledges it before letting it go again. The RED BALLOON floats just out of PASCAL's reach.

Balloon, Red Balloon!

Once more, the RED BALLOON glides down to PASCAL. PASCAL holds its string and they set off to school, at a good pace. Suddenly, the RED BALLOON breaks free, and gets well ahead of PASCAL. It waits for him to catch up. PASCAL

*insists that the RED BALLOON fly back to him. The RED
BALLOON, after a couple of false starts, does so. But just
when PASCAL thinks he'll be able to grab it, it flies over his
head and waits some distance behind him. PASCAL gestures
for it to follow. The RED BALLOON obliges, and settles
behind PASCAL – level with his head. PASCAL takes four
steps forward, and the RED BALLOON copies him. PASCAL
turns to check what the RED BALLOON is doing and the
RED BALLOON floats up high. PASCAL pretends not to
have seen it, and turns back. The RED BALLOON floats
down, right down to the ground. PASCAL stops and bends
over to look for the RED BALLOON through his legs (in
other words he has anticipated what the RED BALLOON is
up to). The RED BALLOON is at PASCAL's back again,
and they set off. Five or six steps this time, before the RED
BALLOON decides to hide, behind a bin, in a doorway,
wherever. PASCAL looks behind him, in front, to the left and
right, turns around looking up, turns around looking down,
and in front of him again, and behind, just as the RED
BALLOON reveals itself. PASCAL tries to grab it, but the
RED BALLOON leads him in a zigzag path, and then around
in a circle, until it looks as though the RED BALLOON is
chasing PASCAL. PASCAL trips and falls. As he is getting
up, the RED BALLOON bumps him on the bottom, and
PASCAL collapses again. PASCAL gets up and watches the
RED BALLOON bobbing up and down. It would seem to be
laughing at him.*

PASCAL: (*Grabbing at the RED BALLOON, unsuccessfully.*)
Be careful or you'll burst!

[M21]

Don't get lost in the wind,
Don't get caught in a tree,
Don't cross the road on your own.
Whatever you do,
Stay close to me –
You're not to be trusted alone.

The RED BALLOON flies back to PASCAL's side, and they both set off again. A CROWD, from different directions, populate the area. If anyone cared to notice, the RED BALLOON is walking beside PASCAL without being held. Nobody notices apart from one CHILD, who is dragged away by a grown-up.

ALL

Every hour of the day taken care of,
Every minute we've something to do.
We haven't the time, the will or the way
To stop what we're doing today.

The RED BALLOON decides to have some fun. It lands on a BAKER's basket of bread. Now the basket is too heavy, or maybe he cannot see where he is going, and he trips, sending the bread flying. The RED BALLOON flies to observe a WOMAN putting on her lipstick. It bounces her arm and she streaks her face red. The RED BALLOON moves on to where TWO WOMEN and a MAN are arguing. When the MAN points to the RED BALLOON in an attempt to distract the WOMEN, because he has been in the wrong, the RED BALLOON biffs him one, and sends him 'seeing stars' to the ground. The RED BALLOON then settles on the stomach of a woman walking arm in arm with her partner. She now looks pregnant, and her partner is shocked and leaves her. The RED BALLOON flies away in the opposite direction, where the TRAMP is just about to sneeze. He does so, and the RED BALLOON lands at his feet. It appears to the TRAMP as though it has shot from his nose. He faints and a WOMAN near by shrieks and jumps into the arms of an unsuspecting PASSER-BY. The RED BALLOON, having gained everybody's attention, floats away.

[M22]

PASCAL (*Letting go of the RED BALLOON.*)

When I let you go
You'll fly,

Fly far away.
Beautiful balloon,
Come back,
Stay close to me.
When I let you go,
Always
Fly back to me.

My balloon, red balloon

The RED BALLOON flies back to PASCAL.

My magic red balloon.

PASCAL lets go of the RED BALLOON, and it flies away to entertain the CROWD.

People passing by
Look up.
They stare at you,
Wonder in their eyes –
What magic
Is holding you there?
People passing by
Reach up
To play with you.

My balloon, red balloon

The RED BALLOON flies back to PASCAL.

My magic red balloon.

As you dance in the sky,
As you swoop, twist and turn,
They wonder who taught you
And how did you learn
The tricks you perform
As you swoop, twist and turn,
As you swoop, twist and turn.

ALL

His balloon, red balloon,
His magic red balloon.

The CROWD become PASSENGERS on the bus, a DRIVER and BUS CONDUCTOR. The GIRL is the last one on the bus.

CONDUCTOR

No dogs, no cats
And no large parcels –

ALL

And definitely, definitely,
Definitely
No gas-filled red balloons.

PASCAL

Nothing in here
Must interfere

With passengers on
      the bus.

When I let you go
You fly far away.

Nothing in here
Must interfere
With passengers on
      the bus.

Red Balloon, come here,
Come back,
Stay close
Behind the bus.

Look, look up, look
Over there!
There, there, there!

We're turning left, we're
       turning right –
Don't lose sight of us,
Keep up with the bus.
My balloon,

We're being followed
By a red balloon!

Red balloon,
My magic red balloon.

Look, look up, look
Over there!
There, there, there!

We're being followed
By a red balloon

How did he tame it?
If only we knew,
Think of the things

We could ask it to do.

The people will swarm
To see you perform
Tricks at the funfair,
Dance in the air!

How did he tame it/
Look, look up,

If only we knew/
Look over there!

Think of the things
We could ask it to do/
Look, look up,
Look over there!
The people will swarm
To see you perform

We're turning left, we're
                turning right
Don't lose sight of us,
Keep up with the bus.

My balloon,
Red balloon
My magic red balloon.

If they ever catch you
They'll never let you go
They will want to tame
                you
And put you on show.

When I let you go

You fly, fly far away.

Red balloon, come here,

Come back,
Stay close to me!

We're being followed
By a red balloon/
Tricks at the funfair,
Dance at the fair!

The balloon, red balloon,
The magic red balloon.
The balloon, red balloon,
THE MAGIC RED BALLOON!

End of Part One

PART TWO

[M23]

Scene Ten

Morning. The school courtyard. The SCHOOL CHILDREN, all similarly dressed in tabliers, enter individually or in small groups to play before school starts. They are gathered together by their LEADER.

CHILDREN

We want to play with
The big red balloon.
If he brings it to school
He must share, that's the rule.
Where's the balloon,
The big red balloon?

PASCAL and the RED BALLOON are discovered outside the school gates, near a large dustbin.

PASCAL

You can't stay at home,
Or come to school and play.
I wish that you,
You could do
Whatever I do –
But rules are rules they say.

PASCAL hides the RED BALLOON in the bin.

Goodbye, Red Balloon,
Be good and wait for me.
I'll be back as soon as I can,
As soon as I'm free.
Be patient and wait here for me.

PASCAL enters the courtyard.

LEADER

Pascal, Pascal,
We want your red balloon.

The CHILDREN surround him.

CHILDREN

Pascal, Pascal,
We want your red balloon.

Pascal, Pascal,
Where is your red balloon?

Pascal, Pascal,
Give us your red balloon.

We want your red balloon,
Give us your red balloon.

*Enter ELAINE. She blows a whistle. Nobody takes any notice.
She blows again. The CHILDREN come to order.*

ELAINE: Good morning, boys and girls.

CHILDREN: Good morning, Mlle Elaine.

ELAINE: Two straight lines.

*ELAINE blows her whistle and the CHILDREN rearrange
themselves in two straight lines. Enter PASCAL. He joins
the back of one line.*

ELAINE: Good morning, Pascal.

PASCAL: Good morning, Mlle Elaine.

*Enter the TRAMP by the school gate, with HERCULE in a
small box under his arm. He lifts the dustbin lid, and the
RED BALLOON escapes with such force that it knocks him
over. The TRAMP lets go of the box and HERCULE escapes.*

TRAMP: (*Crawling away.*) Hercule! Hercule!

The RED BALLOON flies to join PASCAL at the end of the other line. The CHILDREN notice the RED BALLOON, and the two lines break up as they turn and try to grab at it. ELAINE blows her whistle, frantically. The two lines reform. The RED BALLOON waits at a distance.

ELAINE: Pascal?

PASCAL: Yes, Mlle Elaine.

ELAINE: Is that your balloon?

PASCAL: Yes, Mlle Elaine.

CHILDREN turn around to look at the balloon.

ELAINE: What did I say?

PASCAL: Don't be late.

ELAINE: Don't bring toys to school.

PASCAL: I couldn't help it, Mlle Elaine. It follows me everywhere.

ELAINE: You know the rules.

CHILD 1: Please can we play with the balloon.

CHILDREN: Please, Mlle Elaine!/We're allowed./It's not fair./Red Balloon, Red Balloon come here!

The lines break up again, as the CHILDREN rush around the playground trying to catch the RED BALLOON.

PASCAL: It doesn't want to play with you. Leave it alone.

ELAINE: Albert! Albert! (*Blowing her whistle until she is red in the face and waving her arms about like a traffic controller.*)

The lines are re-established. The RED BALLOON makes its way to the front. ELAINE grabs it. The RED BALLOON pulls her to the left, to the right, and then tangles its string in her hair (a full blonde beehive hairdo). It bounces itself three times on her head, in an attempt to free itself, and ELAINE falls to her knees. The RED BALLOON pulls forward, lifting off ELAINE's wig. ELAINE, clinging on to her wig, tries to pull the balloon apart from it. Her actions resemble someone scrubbing the floor, which is what ALBERT sees as he enters. He rushes to her assistance, and starts to scrub the floor with her wig, vigorously. She hits him. The RED BALLOON breaks free, and ALBERT throws the wig into the air. ELAINE catches it.

ELAINE: (*Distraught.*) Save me! Albert, don't be a fool! Save me from that balloon! Save us all!

PASCAL: No, Mlle Elaine, it doesn't want to be locked up all day!

ALBERT stands, sees the RED BALLOON hovering above the CHILDREN, and prepares to lance it with his broom. The RED BALLOON settles amongst the CHILDREN. ALBERT charges at the RED BALLOON. The CHILDREN scream and separate. The RED BALLOON taunts ALBERT. He decides to use his broom as a sword – arm up, he jabs and then cuts at the RED BALLOON twice. As the broom lands on the ground, PASCAL stands on it, and ALBERT lets go. ALBERT, still with the RED BALLOON in sight, has another bright idea. Whipping off his overalls he taunts the RED BALLOON, like a matador holding a red rag to a bull. The RED BALLOON is lured past, and then closer to his overalls. The CHILDREN respond accordingly – gasping, sighing and clapping their support for the RED BALLOON. At the right moment, ALBERT rushes the RED BALLOON with his open overalls, in another attempt to blindfold it. He misses the RED BALLOON and smothers ELAINE.

[M24]

The CHILDREN rush into the classroom as ALBERT is chased away by ELAINE. She uses his broom to frighten him off.

Scene Eleven

The classroom. A large blackboard. Two neat benches. A teacher's chair and small desk.

The CHILDREN put their homework (exercise books) on the teacher's desk. The GIRL last.

PASCAL: (*To the GIRL.*) Can I borrow your homework?

CHILD 4: Don't let him!

The GIRL hesitates, and then puts her homework at the bottom of the pile.

The CHILDREN sit. Enter the RED BALLOON.

ALL: Come here!/Red Balloon! Red Balloon!/ Sit here!/ By me! Not him! Sit by me!/Me! Me! Me!

PASCAL: (*To the RED BALLOON.*) Come here.

The RED BALLOON flies to PASCAL.

PASCAL: Wait outside.

The RED BALLOON doesn't move. Enter ELAINE. CHILDREN stand.

ELAINE: Sit!

The RED BALLOON sits in ELAINE's place. She decides to ignore it.

Today is –

The CHILDREN are distracted by the RED BALLOON.

Does nobody know what day it is?

CHILD 2: Thursday.

ELAINE: Yes, Beatrice. (*Writing Thursday on the blackboard.*) And today's date?

Enter ALBERT with a leaf rake. The RED BALLOON, to avoid him, hovers between the two benches. He stalks it. Standing behind the back bench, he takes a swipe at it. The CHILDREN duck. The RED BALLOON avoids the blow. ALBERT has another go. The CHILDREN duck again, whoop and protest.

PASCAL: No, no, you'll burst it.

ELAINE: (*Ignoring ALBERT and the RED BALLOON.*) And we all know the month, don't we? This is the month of –

GIRL: May.

ELAINE: October.

The RED BALLOON has settled on the floor between the two benches. ALBERT decides to crawl under the bench to get it. He manages to get hold of the RED BALLOON's cord and then is pulled to his feet by the balloon. He is standing on tiptoes and then is yanked forward over the front bench, by the balloon. He topples to the floor, much to the amusement of the CHILDREN.

PASCAL: Red Balloon, come here!

ELAINE: Today's date?

The RED BALLOON settles on ELAINE's bottom as she is writing the month on the blackboard. ALBERT retrieves his broom, and lines himself up to take one final swipe at the balloon. The RED BALLOON flies away just as ALBERT's broom hits ELAINE on the bottom. The CHILDREN laugh. She makes a terrible mess on the board, and then turns to vent her anger on ALBERT. She clobbers the fawning fool with his broom, while the children jeer and cheer. ALBERT rushes from the classroom.

ELAINE blows her whistle. Order is established. The RED BALLOON starts to draw a picture of itself on the blackboard.

ELAINE: Does nobody know today's date?

PASCAL: I do.

ELAINE: Anybody else?

CHILDREN: No, Mademoiselle.
Look at it!/What's it drawing!/What is it?/I know what it is!/The sun./The moon/No it isn't!

ELAINE: All of you! Look at me. Listen. Forget about the balloon. Will you tell me what day it is.

ALL: Thursday.

ELAINE: We know what day it is. The date?

CHILD 3: It's a balloon!

All the CHILDREN cheer, stamp, applaud and demand the RED BALLOON draws something else, as the HEADMASTER and ALBERT enter.

CHILDREN: Draw me!/Draw a house./A cat!/Dog!/Draw a dog!/The Eiffel tower!/Draw the Eiffel tower./Albert! He's fat and round!

HEADMASTER: Silence!

ALL stand in silence.

Sit!

ALL sit, including ELAINE, for a second – before she realises who it is and promptly stands up again.

ELAINE: Good morning, Headmaster.

HEADMASTER: Yes, Mademoiselle Elaine.

ELAINE: (*To the CHILDREN.*) Say 'good morning Headmaster!'

ALBERT: Good morning, Headmaster!

CHILDREN: Good morning, Headmaster!

HEADMASTER: (*To PASCAL.*) You, boy! Stand!

PASCAL stands.

Well may you hang your head, Lamorisse. Is that your balloon?

PASCAL: Yes.

ELAINE: He won't get it out of here. I told him not to bring it to school. He knows the rules. And now none of us can get rid of it. It is disrupting my class. It would seem it has a life of its own.

HEADMASTER: Pascal, come here. Come with me. You know the rules. You don't bring your toys to school. What is that balloon doing here?

PASCAL: It didn't want to be left behind. It didn't want to be left on its own.

HEADMASTER: The truth, Pascal.

PASCAL: It doesn't always do what I tell it to.

CHILD 3: It does.

CHILD 4: He's tamed it.

CHILDREN: It does! He's tamed it! It's magic!

ELAINE: Quiet!

HEADMASTER: Silence!

ELAINE collapses. Head in hands. Distraught.

HEADMASTER: You can stay in my room until you are ready to tell the truth. I've an important meeting to attend at the Town Hall. When I come back I want the truth.

The HEADMASTER walks PASCAL out of the classroom. The RED BALLOON follows.

ELAINE: That wretched red balloon!

ALBERT, to assist Mlle ELAINE, wipes the blackboard clean.

ALBERT: What balloon? Can I see a balloon? I can't see a balloon. (*To the class.*) Can you see a balloon?

CHILDREN: No, Monsieur Albert.

ELAINE: (*Giving ALBERT a withering look.*) Blockhead!

ALBERT: Darling –

ELAINE: Chump.

ALBERT: – heart.

CHILDREN: Chump!

ELAINE: Class dismissed!

The classroom empties.

[M25]

Scene Twelve

The courtyard, and the street.

ALBERT rushes to catch up with the HEADMASTER. The HEADMASTER locks PASCAL in his office. The BALLOON watches, and notes where the key is put – the HEADMASTER's pocket.

HEADMASTER: You can wait in here, until I get back from the Town Hall.

PASCAL: But why –

HEADMASTER: You know why.

PASCAL: I don't.

HEADMASTER: You do.

PASCAL: For how long?

HEADMASTER: Until you can explain to me what that balloon is doing here.

PASCAL: I can't help it. It follows me everywhere.

HEADMASTER: If you expect me to believe that, you must think I'll believe anything.

PASCAL: It's true.

HEADMASTER: The truth never lies, Pascal. Think it over. We'll be back.

PASCAL: Be careful of my balloon.

The BALLOON flies in front of the HEADMASTER.

HEADMASTER: Which direction is the wind blowing?

ALBERT opens his overalls – they become a sail to establish the direction of the wind.

(*To the RED BALLOON.*) Blow away! We're going *this* way.

ALBERT: But that's the long way, Headmaster, and we're late as it is.

HEADMASTER: Safety first.

ALBERT: I'll protect you.

HEADMASTER: Thank you, Albert, but if we let the wind encourage that balloon, I have a feeling I'll never make the meeting.

They turn. The BALLOON adjusts its sights on the HEADMASTER. ELAINE enters.

[M26]

ELAINE

Monsieur –

HEADMASTER

Elaine?

ELAINE

The balloon –

HEADMASTER

Pascal
Won't break school rules again.
And when I say
He'll spend all day –

ELAINE

You mean –

HEADMASTER & ALBERT

ALL DAY!
Locked in my/his room.

ELAINE: But –

HEADMASTER & ALBERT

He'll learn the hard way!

ALBERT: You don't bring toys to school!

HEADMASTER: And if you do –

ELAINE

But Headmaster,
Please understand,
That balloon's possessed –
It should be burst not banned!

It can't be caught,
It won't be told,
However much
We threaten, shout and scold!

HEADMASTER

Have you gone mad,
Or have you had
A little something
That you shouldn't have?

ELAINE

I've not gone mad.
I haven't had
A moment's peace
From that boy and that beast.

HEADMASTER	ELAINE
Have you gone mad,	I've not gone mad
Or have you had	I haven't had
A little something	A moment's peace
That you shouldn't have?	From that boy and that beast.

Under the strain,
Mademoiselle Elaine,
I take it that you can't explain
Why you let that red balloon
Disrupt your class
And chase you round
        the room?
So let me guess:
Under duress
You break the rules –
It's time you left this school.

ELAINE
No, no, no!
That's not true.

ALBERT
Monsieur, Mademoiselle,
Elaine was only –

HEADMASTER
A balloon can't see,
Can't feel, can't hear,

Can't act, can't move
Independently.
A balloon can't be,

ELAINE
So what I saw –

ALBERT
You didn't see –

Can't think, can't have,

ELAINE
I saw it fly!

Can't have what we call

ALBERT
It can't be true!

Personality.

ELAINE
You saw it too!

ALBERT
It pounced and bounced –

ELAINE
It bumped and thumped –

HEADMASTER
A balloon can't see, can't feel, can't hear,
can't act, can't move independently.

ALBERT
It made me laugh –

ELAINE
So what I saw –

ALBERT
You didn't see!

ELAINE
You saw it too!

ALBERT

No only you –

ELAINE

It frightened me! It wasn't funny!

ALBERT

I've only got these eyes for you!

PASSERS-BY have been attracted to the public confrontation between the HEADMASTER and ELAINE. The RED BALLOON is making fun of the HEADMASTER – behind his back.

ELAINE

Look, behind you, sir.

HEADMASTER

What, behind my back?

ELAINE

It's poking fun –

HEADMASTER

At me?

ELAINE

At you.

ALBERT

At her.

ELAINE

At him.

HEADMASTER

It's not doing anything.
See a doctor.

ELAINE: You don't believe me, do you?

HEADMASTER: The truth doesn't lie.

ELAINE: Albert?

ALBERT: I had to fetch the headmaster, for your own sake. Anyone would have done the same. You'd have done the same for me, wouldn't you?

ELAINE: Don't ever speak to me again.

ALBERT: I knew you would. Darling –

ELAINE: Chump!

ELAINE leaves. HEADMASTER and ALBERT look back at the RED BALLOON, before setting off. The RED BALLOON is still, keeping guard outside the headmaster's door.

After taking a few steps, ALBERT and the HEADMASTER sense the RED BALLOON is following them. As indeed it is. They are not certain though, and continue on their way. They stop suddenly and the RED BALLOON crashes into them. They both think the other has patted them on the bottom. They break apart and accuse each other, in gesture, of 'unnecessary familiarity', as the RED BALLOON floats up high and out of sight. They are about to set off again when the RED BALLOON descends, rapidly and knocks off the HEADMASTER's hat. HEADMASTER turns around. ALBERT bends down to pick up the hat and gets bounced on the bottom by the RED BALLOON. ALBERT nearly loses his balance but manages to retrieve the hat, and place it, firmly, on the HEADMASTER's head in one single movement. The HEADMASTER is blinded and flails about. ALBERT panics because he can't get close enough to the HEADMASTER to fix his hat. Dizzy, the HEADMASTER falls to his knees. ALBERT takes this opportunity to straighten the hat while the RED BALLOON lowers its string into the HEADMASTER's pocket to retrieve the key. The HEADMASTER can see again, just as it looks like the

RED BALLOON is going to get the key. He grabs the cord, which has wound its way into his pocket. He is then lifted up, up, up and up and tugged to the right, to the left and to the right again by the RED BALLOON. ALBERT clings on to the HEADMASTER, fearing he may float away. The RED BALLOON gives one last yank to free the key, and it falls to the ground. As do the HEADMASTER and ALBERT. The HEADMASTER rescues the key, while ALBERT threatens the RED BALLOON, with 'punishing looks' and boar-like grunts. Both look at the RED BALLOON as it slowly descends between them. ALBERT, lining up a punch, misses the RED BALLOON and hits the HEADMASTER.

HEADMASTER

It seems to me
It has to be –

ALBERT (*To RED BALLOON.*)

You want to irritate.

HEADMASTER & ALBERT

The games you play,
It seems to us,
Seem quite deliberate.

Fly, fly away,
Leave us alone –
We've got no time to play.

ALBERT

I'm not a child –

HEADMASTER

I've got my work –

ALBERT

His most important work to do.

The RED BALLOON continues to taunt, distract and play with the HEADMASTER and ALBERT. A crowd of

PASSERS-BY are engaged by the spectacle of a couple of supposedly upright citizens being made to look foolish. They laugh and applaud, and sing in round.

CHORUS 1

Bravo, Balloon,
Encore, encore –
We've never seen
The like of this before!
Bravo, Balloon,
Encore, encore –
We've never seen
The like of this before!

CHORUS 2

Don't stop, don't stare –
It's rude to stare.
Don't ever get
Involved out there.
Don't stop, don't stare –
It's rude to stare.
Don't ever get
Involved out there.

CHORUS 3

Did you see that?
It flicked his hat.
He's playing snatch.
It's hard to catch.

These three choruses continue and are joined by Chorus 4 and Albert.

ALBERT	CHORUS 4
Try to ignore it,	What's going on?
Headmaster –	What's happening
It must not bother you.	And what is that
You have too much	Supposed to be?
Important work to do!	What's going on?

The people here
Who stop and stare,
You must ignore them too.
Don't give them time
To laugh and smile at you.

What's happening?
And what is that
Supposed to be?

HEADMASTER

I've lost my cool,
I feel a fool,
I've never felt so small.
They think I'm mad,
Can't act my age –
I'm only mad with rage.

CHORUS

He's only mad with rage!

HEADMASTER

I'll take it back,
No questions asked.
I do not want to know!
Release our prisoner!

CHORUS

Release the prisoner!

*The HEADMASTER and ALBERT retrace their steps –
dragged backwards by the RED BALLOON.*

ALBERT & HEADMASTER

We say, we say,
There is a way
They can communicate.
The games they play,
They seem to us,
Seem quite deliberate.
It seems to me
It has to be

CHORUSES 1, 2, 3 & 4

A balloon can't be,
Can't think, can't act,
Can't fly its mind
Independently.
A balloon can't see,
Can't hear, can't be,
Can't have, can't have
Personality!

You want to irritate.
The games you play,
It seems to us,
Seem quite deliberate.

HEADMASTER

Get out, the pair of you,
Out of my sight!
Don't stop to argue
Who is wrong or who is right!
Just get out of my sight!

CHORUS

Just get out of his sight!

ALBERT

Get out the pair of you,
Out of our sight!
Don't say
Whatever you think –
What you think won't be right!

CHORUS

What you think won't be right!

HEADMASTER & ALBERT

Not a moment too soon
To be rid of them both,
That boy
And his great big balloon!

(*X2 with the last line repeated twice again with a three-part chorus.*)

CHORUS 1

Bravo, Balloon,
Encore, encore –
We've never seen
The like of this before!

CHORUS 2

Don't stop, don't stare –
It's rude to stare.
Don't ever get
Involved out there.

CHORUS 3

Did you see that?
It flicked his hat.
He's playing snatch.
It's hard to catch.

CHORUS 4

What's going on?
What's happening?
And what is that
Supposed to be?

ALL

Bravo, Balloon,
Bravo, bravo,
Bravo, bravo,
Bravo, Balloon!

The HEADMASTER unlocks his office door to free PASCAL. PASCAL and the RED BALLOON walk away as the PASSERS-BY disperse. Enter the GIRL.

GIRL: Where's the red balloon gone?

Enter CHILDREN.

HEADMASTER: Gone, gone –

CHILD 2: Where?

HEADMASTER & ALBERT: Gone.

HEADMASTER: If I ever see that balloon again, I'll...I'll... I'll sit on it.

ALBERT: If the headmaster ever sees that balloon again he'll sit on it.

CHILD 3: No you won't.

HEADMASTER and ALBERT leave.

[M27]

CHILDREN

We want to play with
The big red balloon!
If he brings it to school
He must share, that's the rule.
Where's the balloon,
The big red balloon?

CHILD 1

I know what!

CHILD 3

What?

CHILD 2

Come over here!

CHILD 1

I know where he's taken it!

CHILDREN 2, 3, 4 & 5

Where?

CHILD 1

Taken it –

CHILD 2

Home!

CHILD 5

To the shop.

CHILD 3

To the market.

CHILD 4

To church.

CHILDREN 2 & 3

To the river.

CHILD 3

TO THE MARKET!

CHILDREN

Wherever they are,
They can't have gone far.
The balloon all alone...
We will creep up behind him/it –
We'll push/we'll grab,
We'll punch/hold tight,
Let us have a go/and we'll never let go,
Never, never let go.
If we spread out,
We'll find it,
We'll find it.
They'll never escape,
Never, never escape.
We'll find it, we'll find it!
We'll bring it back here,
We'll make it do those tricks in the air.
Pascal, Pascal,
Give us your balloon,
Give us your big red balloon,
Or we'll never be your friend again,
Never, never be your friend again!

The CHILDREN rush away in different directions, but the majority to the market.

Enter PASCAL and the RED BALLOON.

[M28]

PASCAL

I can't take you home,
And we can't stay at school –
What are we going to do?
If only I knew
How to put it to you,
You'd do what I tell you to do.

Don't get lost in the wind,
Don't get caught in a tree,
Don't fly away on your own.
Wherever I go,
You stay close to me –
You're not to be trusted alone.

[M29]

Scene Thirteen

An old flea market is established around PASCAL and the RED BALLOON – SELLERS and BUYERS. There is a cycle stall, a bric-a-brac cart, a picture postcard and paintings stall (which is selling a large oval picture of a little girl in a white dress, with a hoop), and a stall selling old clothes, a couple of rails full. PASCAL and the RED BALLOON wander around the market.

ALL

In this market of memories
You're bound to find
A present of somebody's past.
Old things forgotten
Are here to remind you –
The future is yours to define.

BUYER 1

Will you take this for that?

BUYER 2

I can't afford more!

BUYER 3

Does it still work?

BUYER 4

Has it been used before?

BUYER 5

But isn't it lovely!

SELLER 1

And so hard to ignore!

ALL

Something I don't need
But will use, I'm sure.

*PASCAL at the cycle stall. The RED BALLOON dissuades
PASCAL from buying an old bicycle.*

CYCLE SELLER

This cycle here,
It needs slight repair –
For the price of a dream,
It's yours.

PASCAL

Monsieur, my balloon
Knows it's not right
For you to sell me that bike.

It's going nowhere –

CYCLE SELLER

It'll soon ride again –

PASCAL

Without wheels and a chain –

CYCLE SELLER

Like a bird on the wing –

PASCAL

Its saddle is broken –

CYCLE SELLER

And race you to places –

PASCAL

Its handlebars sprained –

CYCLE SELLER

That you've never been.

PASCAL

I'll give you one franc
For that frame.

CYCLE SELLER

One franc for this bike –
What's your game?

PASCAL and the RED BALLOON move on.

SELLERS

In this market of memories –

BUYERS

Will you take this for that –

SELLERS

You're bound to find –

BUYERS

I can't afford more –
Does it still work?

SELLERS

A present of somebody's past.

BUYERS

Has it been used before?
But isn't it lovely –

SELLERS

Old things forgotten
Are here to remind you –

BUYERS

And so hard to ignore.
Something I don't need –

SELLERS

The future is yours to define.

BUYERS

But will use, I'm sure.

PASCAL and the RED BALLOON at the picture stall.

PICTURE SELLER

Don't you know this picture
Was painted for you?
By an old master,
Who knew that you'd met
The girl with the hoop
And the short brown hair,
In your daydreams, at night
When you're down to despair.
Who runs and hides
When you want to play.
I'll sell you this picture,
Then she won't run away.

PASCAL

How much does it cost?

PICTURE SELLER

How much have you got?

PASCAL

No one will want it,
It was painted for me!

The picture of the GIRL in the white dress comes to life.

PICTURE SELLER

Show me your money,
And then let me see.

PASCAL

I'll give you one franc,
If you take it home for me.

PICTURE SELLER

One franc for that picture?

ALL

Huh! Robbery!

PASCAL and the RED BALLOON move on. The painting dissolves, and from behind it appears the GIRL with a hoop. She follows PASCAL, and rushes off, chasing her hoop. He never sees her.

SELLERS

In this market of memories –

BUYERS

Will you take this for that –

SELLERS

You're bound to find –

BUYERS

I can't afford more –
Does it still work?

SELLERS

A present of somebody's past.

BUYERS

Has it been used before?
But isn't it lovely –

SELLERS

Old things forgotten
Are here to remind you –

BUYERS

And so hard to ignore.
Something I don't need –

SELLERS

The future is yours to define.

BUYERS

But will use, I'm sure.

PASCAL and the RED BALLOON find a PHOTOGRAPHER.

PASCAL

Please take a photograph
Of me and my balloon.
I want to have a picture
To hang up in my room.

PHOTOGRAPHER

Show me your money,
And then let us see –

PASCAL

I'll give you one franc,
If you'll take it for me –

PHOTOGRAPHER

One franc for my magic!
You can have it for free!

PASCAL

Red Balloon, fly still
While I comb my hair.
Shine your big red face
In the breeze up there.

PHOTOGRAPHER

Please stand very still
And look up at your balloon.

Smile at that face
In the big red moon.

As PASCAL prepares for the photograph, enter the GIRL and the BLUE BALLOON.

A flash. PASCAL waits for the plate in the box camera to develop. The RED BALLOON flies off to make the acquaintance of the BLUE BALLOON. The GIRL is anxious about the RED BALLOON's advances.

The PHOTOGRAPHER hands PASCAL the photo. When he sees it, PASCAL realises that the GIRL with the BLUE BALLOON has been caught by the camera.

                              ALL

In this market of memories
You're bound to find
A present of somebody's past.
Old things forgotten
Are here to remind you –
The future is yours to define.

The BUYERS and SELLERS disperse, taking the market with them.

                          [M30]

Scene Fourteen

The street.

PASCAL: Hello.

GIRL: Where did you get your balloon?

PASCAL: I found it.

GIRL: I like blue.

PASCAL: Let it go.

GIRL: No. I'll lose it. I don't want to lose my balloon.

PASCAL: Balloon, Red Balloon!

GIRL: Why doesn't it fly away?

PASCAL: It's magic. All I have to do is call, and it comes floating back to me.

GIRL: Show me.

PASCAL: Balloon. Balloon. Red Balloon. Come here.

The RED BALLOON disobeys. The GIRL laughs.

PASCAL: Don't laugh. You'll see. Balloon. Balloon. Come back. My balloon has the shiniest red face. It can look over the wall and show me what's on the other side.

GIRL: Maman says, because I'm small that wall is tall. But when I'm tall it will be small. When I'm grown up.

PASCAL: Shall we play a game? Can I be your friend?

Enter a CHILD.

GIRL: My friend lives next door.

PASCAL leaves.

CHILD: (*Calling to the group.*) He's over here.

CHILDREN enter.

[M31]

CHILD

Where's he gone?

GIRL

Who?

CHILD

You know who!
Don't pretend that you don't –
I saw you
Talking to him.

CHILDREN

Pascal!

GIRL

He's gone along –

CHILD

Where?

GIRL

He's just gone along.

CHILD

But where is along?

GIRL

Somewhere he's gone.

CHILDREN

We want to play with
The big red balloon!
If he brings it to school
He must share, that's the rule.
Balloon, red balloon,
Where is the red balloon?

CHILD

If you don't tell us,
Then we'll make you pay.
What did he tell you
That you cannot say?

GIRL

You can do what you like –
He said nothing to me.

The CHILDREN surround her, threateningly.

He said nothing except –

CHILDREN

What?

GIRL

His balloon could see.

CHILDREN

See?

GIRL

Over the wall.

CHILDREN

What?

GIRL

He wouldn't tell me.

CHILDREN

If you don't tell us,
We'll force you to say.
We'll burst your balloon,
We'll let it fly away.

Balloon, balloon,
Where is the red balloon?

GIRL

All of you go home,
Leave me alone.
All of you go home, go home.
If you burst my balloon,
I will tell Mademoiselle –

CHILDREN

We'll pull your hair,
And pretend you're not there.
We'll call you names,
And leave you out of our games.

Balloon, balloon,
We'll burst your
Blue balloon!

Tell us, tell us
What he said to you.
Tell us, tell us
What the red balloon can do.

Tell us, tell us,
Or we'll never play with you.
Tell us, tell us –

CHILD

OR WE'LL BURST YOUR BLUE
BALLOON.

Tell us, tell me,
Before I count to three,
Or we'll never be your friend again,
Never, never be your friend again.

CHILDREN

One!
Two!
Two and a half –

The RED BALLOON appears over the wall.

CHILDREN

Look, look up,
Look over there –
There, there, there.
Red balloon, red balloon,
We want the red balloon.

How did he tame it?
If only we knew –
Think of the things we could ask it to do.

*The RED BALLOON distracts the CHILDREN. The GIRL
runs away with her BLUE BALLOON. Enter PASCAL.*

PASCAL

Red Balloon, come here,
Come back,
Stay close to me.
Red Balloon, come here,
Come back,
Stay close to me.

*The RED BALLOON flies back to the safe hands of PASCAL.
PASCAL rushes off.*

The angry CHILDREN leave in various directions.

Scene Fifteen

On another street in Paris. PASCAL and his RED BALLOON.

PASCAL: Why did you do that? I wanted to show her that
you were magic, and you didn't do what I said. Why
not? Why won't you do what I tell you to? It's not fair.
I'll let you go. I will. I'll just let you go.

*PASCAL releases the RED BALLOON, but it doesn't fly
away. PASCAL turns his back on the RED BALLOON.
The RED BALLOON makes overtures to be accepted again.
PASCAL, finally, agrees. Enter the GIRL and the BLUE
BALLOON. They stop and stare at each other in silence.
The BALLOONS want to make friends.*

[M32]

PASCAL

Red and blue,
I'd like to spend this time with you,
Red and blue.

GIRL

If we haven't met –

PASCAL

We should have done.

GIRL

If I didn't say –

PASCAL

I wanted to –

GIRL

Ask you
What you do –

PASCAL

Would you like to –

TOGETHER

Shhh !
I can't expect you to.

GIRL

Red and blue,
I'd like to spend this time with you.

TOGETHER

Lost at you looking at me,
Knowing you feel differently.
Whatever I feel, you have never felt,
Felt for me, what I feel for you.
No hello, no goodbye,
But we'll let the hope fly –
Red balloon meets blue, in the sky.

The RED and BLUE BALLOONS dance.

A CHILD's face appears from behind the wall.

Red and blue,
The time I could have spent with you,
RED AND BLUE.

CHILD 3

There it is! Over there!

105

PASCAL escapes with his RED BALLOON. CHILDREN appear from a number of directions.

CHILD 5: Have you seen the red balloon?

GIRL: No.

CHILD 4 stands back with a catapult aimed at the BLUE BALLOON.

CHILD 3: I saw you. You were talking to him. It was here. Where did it go?

GIRL: (*Releasing her BLUE BALLOON.*) Fly away, fly away or they'll burst you.

CHILD 1: You've lost your balloon.

GIRL: No I haven't. Blue Balloon! Blue Balloon!

GIRL runs after her BLUE BALLOON.

CHILD 4: You're not going anywhere, until you tell us which way he went.

GIRL: (*Pointing.*) That way.

The pack of CHILDREN confer. The GIRL takes the opportunity to escape.

[M33]

CHILDREN

Red Balloon, Red Balloon,
We want the Red Balloon.
Red Balloon, Red Balloon,
We want the Red Balloon.
Red Balloon, Red Balloon,
We want the Red Balloon.

The CHILDREN leave.

Scene Sixteen

The street, and sweetshop. A large CHILD emerges from the sweetshop, carrying a bag or jar of sweets – sucking a lollipop in the shape of the RED BALLOON, perhaps.

Enter PASCAL and the RED BALLOON.

PASCAL: (*To the RED BALLOON.*) Wait here. I'm hungry. I'm just going into the shop to buy some chocolate.

The RED BALLOON is on its own. It wriggles into the sun. The CHILDREN appear. In silence they stalk the RED BALLOON. The RED BALLOON wriggles, nervously. If it is to obey PASCAL it must wait. The CHILDREN steal the BALLOON, tie it to a long string/light rope and drag it off.

PASCAL comes out of the shop.

PASCAL: Red Balloon. Red Balloon. What did I tell you? Why don't you ever do what I say? Red Balloon! Red Balloon!

PASCAL rushes off in search of the RED BALLOON. The music has kept building. Enter CHILDREN dragging the RED BALLOON like a bull, or a stubborn donkey, through the streets. They beat the ground behind the RED BALLOON, and threaten it with sharp sticks. This journey is savage – cruel. The CHILDREN drive the RED BALLOON into a clearing and the music stops. They try to instruct the RED BALLOON. The RED BALLOON contradicts their commands.

CHILD 2 performs a dance.

CHILD 1: Dance.

CHILDREN: Dance, dance, dance!

The RED BALLOON is motionless.

CHILDREN 3 & 4: (*Demonstrate skipping.*) Skip! Skip!

CHILD 1 does a handstand. CHILD 5 lifts CHILD 1 on his/her shoulders.

Other CHILDREN cartwheel, contort and make faces, but the RED BALLOON remains unresponsive. CHILD 5 threatens the RED BALLOON with a sharp stick. The GIRL enters.

GIRL: Don't, you'll burst it!

They all turn to the GIRL.

CHILD 1: You tell it to do something.

CHILD 5: It's lost it.

PASCAL on a different level or from behind a wall.

PASCAL: RED BALLOON! RED BALLOON!

The RED BALLOON flies to PASCAL. The CHILDREN scramble to get the rope, in order not to lose the RED BALLOON. A tug of war ensues between the CHILDREN and PASCAL/BALLOON. The RED BALLOON gets the better of them. PASCAL unties the long rope, and the CHILDREN fall back like a row of dominoes. PASCAL and the RED BALLOON rush off as the CHILDREN pour over the wall, in hot pursuit. The chase is on.

CHILD 4: It's gone. Escaped. Quick.

CHILD 1: It's Pascal. He's got it.

CHILD 3: After him. Quick. Run.

CHILDREN: (*Chant.*) Balloon, Red Balloon, we want the Red Balloon.

CHILD 2: Cut him off. That way.

CHILD 1: Drive him onto the waste ground.

CHILD 3: He's gone down that way. Over there!

CHILD 5: Get him, Beatrice.

CHILD 2: Zazu, run. Run, Zazu, run!

The CHILDREN run off and PASCAL and the RED BALLOON reappear from a different direction.

PASCAL

Don't get lost in the wind,
Don't get caught in a tree,

Don't cross the road on your own.
Whatever you do,
Stay close to me –
They'll catch you when you're on your own.

*The CHILDREN reappear ready to ambush PASCAL and
the RED BALLOON.*

CHILDREN

Look, look up, look over there –
Red Balloon, come here.

There, there, Red Balloon,
Red Balloon, come here.

How did he tame it? If only we knew,
Think of the things we could ask it to do.

*ALL running through the streets of Paris. PASCAL and the
RED BALLOON manage to avoid getting caught. An OLD
WOMAN with a large basket of bread, negotiating a narrow
alley, holds up the CHILDREN as PASCAL slips through.
When the chase can get no faster, the action freezes. Silhouetted
against a stormy sky are PASCAL and the RED BALLOON.*

ALL

The wind chased the clouds across the sky
While the sea drowned the sand on the shore.
The sun chased the moon into the day
While winter chased summer away.

Run, run, run, Pascal.
Red Balloon, fly away. (*Repeated.*)

The stories that matter to me and to you
Are the dreams that we dream come true!

CHILD 1: (*Pointing to PASCAL and the RED BALLOON.*)
There they are, they're over there.

*PASCAL and the RED BALLOON run for it. Believing they
have escaped the pack, PASCAL collapses on a piece of
wasteground. SILENCE. The sun starts to set. Suddenly the
CHILDREN run in from every direction. They surround
PASCAL. They point their catapults at the RED BALLOON.
All except the GIRL. Then the CHILDREN threaten her
with their catapults until she agrees to raise her own against
PASCAL. PASCAL stands, fearful.*

PASCAL: Fly away! Fly away! Don't let them burst you.

*He lets go of the RED BALLOON. The RED BALLOON
floats away above the heads of the CHILDREN. This time
instead of turning to chase the balloon, they aim their catapults
at PASCAL. The RED BALLOON, from a little way off,
sees what's going on and comes back, to protect PASCAL. The
CHILDREN fire their catapults at the RED BALLOON,
and they burst it.*

*The CHILDREN slope off, some proud of what they have
done, others ashamed.*

[M34]

PASCAL

When I call balloon
In an empty room,
Search the air,
Expecting you there,
I will find the time that we used to share
Passes so slow, because you're not there.

(*Sax solo.*)

Will you follow me,
Like you used to do?
Will I call your name
Over again,
Jump on your shadow and dodge the rain?
Can we fly through the streets of Paris again?

I will miss you,
Red Balloon, I will miss you.
I will miss you,
Red Balloon, I will miss you.

[M35]

THE REVOLT OF THE BALLOONS. Balloons appear from all directions, singly, in pairs, threes, fours, in a group. They never stop coming. All the balloons in Paris.

Enter twelve or more OPERATOR/PUPPETEERS, who gather the balloons. They entwine their balloon strings and hand them to PASCAL. Soon PASCAL is holding a parachute of balloons so vast, that it only takes one more balloon – a red balloon – to lift him off the ground and up. Up over Paris and away.

ALL

My balloon, red balloon,

My magic RED BALLOON.

The End.

Encore [M36]